TALL TALL TREE

By Anthony D. Fredericks
Illustrated by Chad Wallace

Dawn Publications

For Anthony and Allison DeSantis
May their world be filled with lots of tall tall adventures and great great discoveries.—ADF

For my Godson Jackson.—CW

Library of Congress Cataloging-in-Publication Data

Names: Fredericks, Anthony D. | Wallace, Chad, illustrator.
Title: Tall, tall tree / by Anthony D. Fredericks ; illustrated by Chad
  Wallace.
Description: First edition. | Nevada City, CA : Dawn Publications, [2017] |
  Audience: Ages 3-8. | Audience: K to grade 3.
Identifiers: LCCN 2016046842| ISBN 9781584696018 (hardcover) | ISBN
  9781584696025 (pbk.)
Subjects: LCSH: Cloud forest animals--Juvenile literature. | Forest
  animals--Juvenile literature. | Forest canopies--Juvenile literature.
Classification: LCC QL112 .F734 2017 | DDC 591.734--dc23
LC record available at https://lccn.loc.gov/2016046842

Book design and computer production by Patty Arnold, *Menagerie Design & Publishing*

Manufactured by Regent Publishing Services, Hong Kong,
Printed April 2019 in ShenZhen, Guangdong, China

10 9 8 7 6 5 4 3 2

First Edition

Dawn Publications
12402 Bitney Springs Road
Nevada City, CA 95959
800-545-7475
www.dawnpub.com

Dear Humans:

I live at the top of a tree—a tall, tall tree! My tree is a redwood, one of the tallest trees in the world. Redwoods are higher than many buildings. That's really tall! This tree is where I find my food. It's also where I sleep and raise my family. And, it's where I hide from animals who want to catch me.

There are lots of other animals who live up here, too. Some live here their entire lives. Some just visit for a little while. And some come and go throughout the year.

Yet, for a long time, scientists didn't know where we lived. They didn't think we could live so high. This was our hidden world. Finally, people learned how to climb these tall trees. When they did, they discovered us. Imagine their surprise! They also learned something new. Because we live so high, sometimes our weather up here is different than your weather down there. Isn't that amazing?

So, welcome to our special place—our redwood tree! There are a lot of amazing things to discover here; a lot to learn. By learning more, you can help save and protect our fragile ecosystem. And we could sure use your help! In fact, we'll count on it.

Wisely Yours,

Northern Spotted Owl

Creeping, hopping, zipping
Throughout the redwoods green
Are many different creatures
Who are very seldom seen.

They live among the branches
High in this tall, tall tree,
Insects, birds, and mammals,
Let's count them—**one, two, three**.

1
One

A single soaring Eagle
Against a sky of blue,
Searches for his dinner,
And now comes number...

2
Two

Two brown and spotted Owls
Nest in the canopy,
Carrying food to babies,
And now comes number…

3
Three

Three climbing Salamanders
Above the forest floor,
Hunt for tiny insects,
And now comes number...

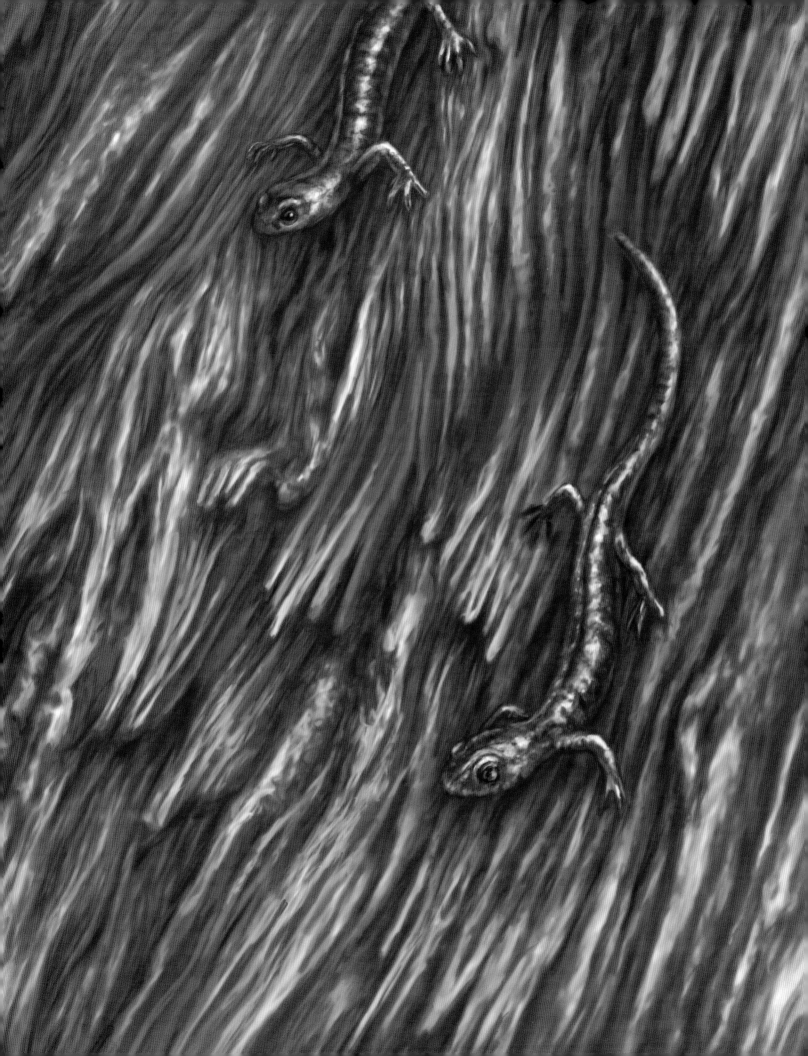

4
Four

Four busy Woodpeckers,
In order to survive,
Are storing all their acorns,
And now comes number…

5
Five

Five furry Woodrats,
Darting in the sticks,
Dining on some juicy plants,
And now comes number...

6
Six

Six chattering Chipmunks,
In this tree-top heaven,
Dash, dart, and scamper,
And now comes number…

7
Seven

Seven busy Bumblebees
Zig and zag and wait.
They flash in black and yellow,
And now comes number...

8
Eight

Eight sleeping Bats
Roosting in a line,
Waiting for the moon to rise,
And now comes number…

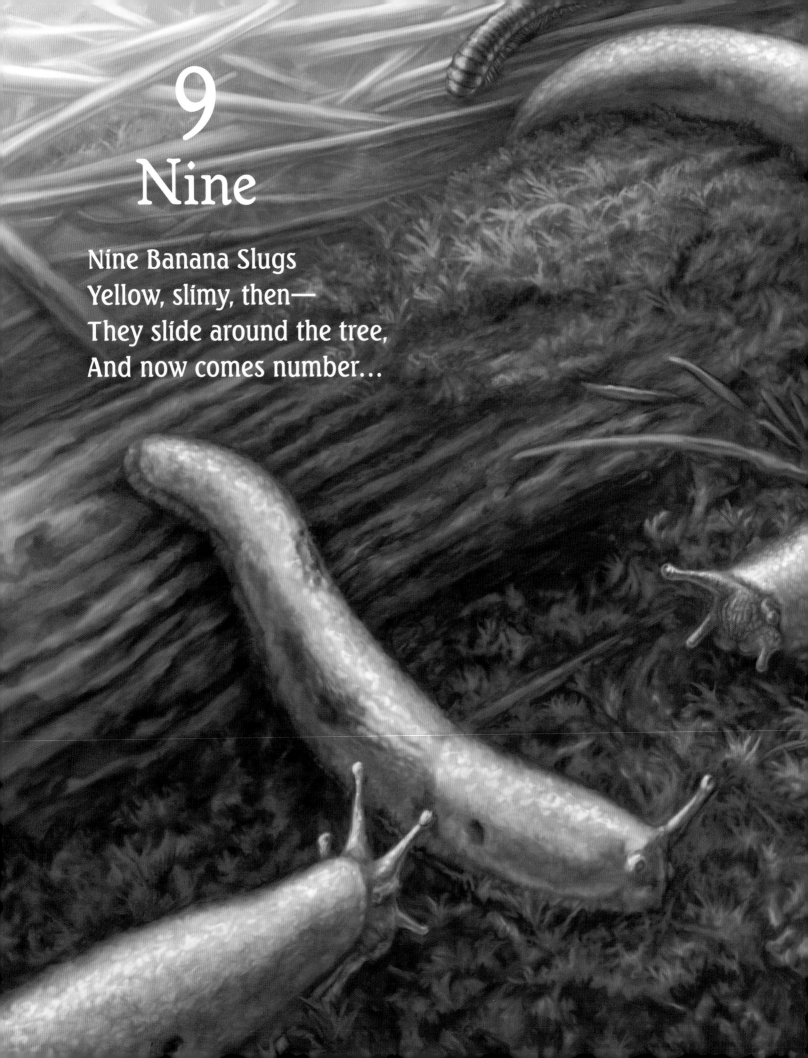

9
Nine

Nine Banana Slugs
Yellow, slimy, then—
They slide around the tree,
And now comes number…

10
Ten

Ten spotted Ladybugs,
On teeny tiny feet,
Crawl along the needles,
But our story's not complete.

Many other animals
Sleep and eat and roam
Up in this tall, tall tree —
Their elevated home.

The tree lives in a forest
Close to the foggy shore.
It's a wild and magic world—
Come discover and explore!

Meet the World's Tallest Tree: The Coast Redwood

Tall

Many redwood trees are over 360 feet tall. That's taller than a 30-story skyscraper.

Wide

They're nearly 30 feet wide. That's as wide as a volleyball court.

Only Here

These trees only grow in one place in the world—near the coast of northern California and southern Oregon.

High Home

Needles, bark, and leaves from other trees collect on redwood tree branches. After time, they become mats of spongy humus.

These mats are like gardens in the sky. They allow many plants and animals that live on the ground to also live up high in the treetops.

Ancient

They can be more than 2,000 years old.

Needles

The flat needles of a redwood are its leaves.

Bark

The bark protects the tree from fire and insects. In some spots, the bark may be up to one-foot thick.

Thirsty

Each day a large redwood tree moves hundreds of gallons of water from its roots to its crown.

Roots

The roots spread out more than 50 feet from the trunk. Redwood trees living in a grove intertwine their roots. This helps them stand strong against powerful winds.

Find the Hidden Animals

You've met ten animals (from 1 to 10) that live in and around a redwood tree. Did you see other animals "hiding" in the illustrations? Look closely for these critters. Some of them only show a part of themselves:

Paper Wasps—These wasps make hanging nests created of thin paper-like sheets. To make the sheets, wasps mix plant material with their saliva!

Yellow-spotted Millipede—This critter has 62 legs. (Wow! That's a lot of legs!) Millipedes like to eat fallen leaves, which they convert into rich topsoil. The topsoil is necessary for forest plants to grow.

California Sister Butterfly—You might see this butterfly fluttering through the forest. Like all butterflies, they don't bite or chew their food because they don't have mouths—they just suck it up.

Northern Flying Squirrel—This type of squirrel doesn't really fly. It glides from tree to tree going as far as 50 yards. That's half a football field! But on the ground they are very clumsy walkers.

Wandering Salamander—Scientists thought these 5-inch long critters only lived on the ground. Imagine their surprise when they discovered these animals living high up on humus mats.

Skunk—Whew! Skunks can shoot out their stinky spray as far as ten feet. That keeps away a lot of predators. They are mostly active at night, when they search for food.

Red Tree Vole—Related to rats, these voles live only in northern California and Oregon. They like to eat conifer needles. Owls, on the other hand, like to eat voles.

Marbled Murrelet—Even though it's a seabird, this murrelet nests high in redwood trees. Murrelets spend most of their time at the ocean where they dive underwater to catch fish.

Allen's Hummingbird—About 3-inches long, this tiny bird mostly lives along the California coast. Like all hummingbirds, it can fly backwards, upside-down, and hover in mid-air.

Steller's Jay—This bold bird isn't afraid of people. It will swoop down from the trees to steal food from a picnic table. Look for its blue feathers and listen for its loud call.

Tiny to Gigantic

A tall, tall tree grows from a tiny, tiny seed. A redwood seed is about the same size as a tomato seed. Over its lifetime, a redwood tree may make a billion seeds, sometimes more! Seeds develop inside a small cone. Redwood trees also sprout from stumps, tree roots, and burls. The tallest coast redwood tree is about 380 feet.

Redwood Seed

●

Actual Size

Amazing Redwood Trees!

On a recent vacation, my wife and I traveled to northern California to explore the trees of Redwood National and State Parks. We were amazed by these titans—botanical kings soaring skyward in splendid groves tucked into verdant valleys and along sinuous trails. I was there to conduct some research for this book and gathered a remarkable volume of information. For example:

» The first redwood fossils date back to the Jurassic period (when the dinosaurs were around).

» These trees can live for more than 2,000 years. Several redwoods alive today were also living during the Roman Empire.

» The world's tallest tree in Redwood National Park is called Hyperion. It is about 380 feet tall—nearly six stories taller than the Statue of Liberty.

» A redwood tree may weigh as much as 26 blue whales or 765 African elephants!

Here I am at the park dwarfed by a fallen redwood.

Discovering Gardens in the Sky

Until the late 1980s, redwoods were thought to be so tall that no animals could possibly live in their high branches. It wasn't until Stephen Sillett (now a professor at Humboldt State University) and a small group of brave adventurers ascended these towering giants that a previously unexplored world of creatures was discovered. As Sillett ventured high into the canopy he observed how crotches and limbs high up in the canopy trapped falling needles and other debris. This material formed humus mats up to 265 feet above the ground. These elevated mats became habitats for many animals typically found on the forest floor.

Many creatures live in and around one tall, tall (redwood) tree, including these from the story:

» **Bald Eagles**—With a wingspan of over eight feet long, eagles soar above the treetops searching for food.

» **Northern Spotted Owls**—Living in old-growth forests, these owls like to nest in trees with large holes, deformed limbs, or broken tops.

» **Clouded Salamanders**—These amphibians will climb up and down redwood trees in search of ants, mites, and other small insects to eat.

» **Acorn Woodpeckers**—These woodpeckers are known for storing acorns in small holes they drill into tree trunks—redwood bark works very well.

» **Dusky-footed Woodrats**—Also called "pack rats" because they collect lots of small items, these rodents may live together in large stick houses.

» **Yellow-cheeked Chipmunks**—Because these animals usually live on the ground, it was a surprising discovery to find them living on humus mats high in the canopy.

» **Bumblebees**—Huckleberry bushes are one of the bushes that grow on humus mats. Bumblebees are necessary pollinators of huckleberries.

» **Big Brown Bats**—These mammals live in the basal hollows of old-growth redwoods where there are stable temperatures for the colonies throughout the year.

» **Banana Slugs**—Slugs (often 7–9 inches long) consume dead plant material, animal droppings, and moss. They live alone, except during mating season, when you can find dozens on the forest floor.

» **Lady Beetles**—Also called ladybugs, these beetles are an important part of the redwood forest ecosystem.

STEAM Activities

SCIENCE—Growing Humus Mats

Use information on the previous pages to explain humus mats to your students. Invite students to create their own classroom "spongy" humus mats by placing several old sponges on plastic plates (one sponge per plate). Soak each sponge thoroughly with water and have students sprinkle seeds on top of each one.

Suggested "plantings" include: grass seeds (various varieties), bean seeds, radish seeds (my favorite), carrot seeds, wildflower seeds, or lettuce seeds. Place the plates on a sunny windowsill, keep the sponges well-watered, and invite students to record the growth of their classroom plants over several weeks.

TECHNOLOGY—Let's Visit the Redwoods

Many children and adults may never visit a redwood forest. You can help others appreciate the beauty of this special place and give them important background experience by sharing a YouTube video called "Redwood Forest Relaxation HD Video- Nature Sounds 1080p HD." This 7-minute, 41-second video has no human voices or background music—just the sights and sounds of nature all around. After viewing, ask students what they saw and heard. Then, read this book aloud — inviting students to imagine they are in a redwood forest looking at the animals profiled in the verses and illustrated on the pages. Ask them what else they may have noticed in the redwood forest video. For example, ferns, fallen logs, bushes, trails, or flowers.

ENGINEERING—Marshmallow Towers

Divide the class into small groups. Provide each group with 9 miniature marshmallows and 15 round toothpicks. Invite each group to construct the tallest free-standing structure (may not touch anything) they can by inserting the toothpicks (which simulate branches and trunks) into the marshmallows. What challenges do they encounter? What happens as the structure (tree) gets taller? What is the best "base" (roots) for the structure? What parallels do they note between their structures and tall, tall trees?

ART—Bark Pictures

Bark is an important part of every tree. Redwood bark protects the tree from insects, disease, and fire damage. Help students understand the importance of tree bark by creating bark pictures. Remove the wrappings from several different colored crayons. Provide each student with a crayon and a piece of white paper. Go for a walk with your class and invite them to lay a piece of paper against the bark of a tree. Using the side of a crayon have them rub across the paper. They will begin to see the pattern of the bark appear on the paper. Encourage students to visit other trees to make additional bark rubbings. Give them each a different piece of paper and a different color crayon for each tree. Back in the classroom, compare the patterns, noting any similarities or differences. Explain that even though bark is different from tree to tree, it performs the same function—protecting the tree.

MATH—By the Numbers

Redwood forests harbor lots of animal species:

- More than 60 different mammals
- 13 kinds of bats
- 11 different reptiles
- More than 280 kinds of birds
- Hundreds of insects

Use bookmarks of the animals (available as a free download at dawnpub.com/activities) to practice addition and subtraction. For example: Woodrats plus woodpeckers equal how many animals? Slugs minus salamanders? Add all the birds. Add all of the animals in the book, 1–10. Now add the hidden animals.

Suggested Web Sites

- **Save the Redwoods League**—This group protects redwoods and connects people to their beauty. Lots of information and teacher resources. www.savetheredwoods.org

- **Project Learning Tree**—A complete environmental education program for K-12 teachers. Creative, hands-on, and meets standards. https://www.plt.org

- **The National Park Service**—Provides loads of information about redwood trees. It's a great place to begin making your plans for a visit to these botanical giants. http://www.nps.gov/redw

There are many useful resources online for most of Dawn's books, including activities and standards-based lesson plans. Scan this code to go directly to activities for this book, or go to www.dawnpub.com and click on "Activities" for this and other books.

Anthony D. Fredericks grew up in California and Arizona where he hiked tall mountains and long forest trails. These days Tony explores several wild places in south-central Pennsylvania where he and his wife live. A former classroom teacher and reading specialist, he is now retired as Professor of Education at York College, York, PA. He is a prolific author, having published more than 150 books, including over four dozen children's books on nature and environmental studies. Learn more about Tony's books at www.anthonydfredericks.com.

Chad Wallace is an award-winning artist from Westchester, NY. His illustrations often feature animals in their natural environment or somewhat anthropomorphized. Chad's art is influenced by his experiences growing up in rural Northern Westchester and summers in the Lower Hudson Valley. Chad earned his BFA at Syracuse University and his MFA at the Fashion Institute of Technology, where he serves as an adjunct professor. Chad also holds teaching positions at the New York City College of Technology, and New Jersey City University. This is his 12th book for children, including one he authored.

More Books by Anthony D. Fredericks

Under One Rock: Bugs, Slugs and Other Ughs—One of the world's most fascinating habitats lives right at your feet. No child will be able to resist looking under a rock after reading the rhythmic text and fascinating facts.

Near One Cattail: Turtles, Logs and Leaping Frogs—Zip-zipping dragonflies, hop-hopping frogs, and a medley of other critters invite children to discover the wetlands habitat.

In One Tidepool: Crabs, Snails and Salty Tails— Colorful critters abound once you peer into the water. Readers will get an intriguing glimpse into this salty, splashy habitat.

More Books by Chad Wallace

The Mouse and the Meadow—Experience the vibrant and sometimes dangerous nature of meadow life from a mouse's eye-view. Science blends seamlessly into the story.

Pass the Energy, Please!—Everybody is somebody's lunch. This perennial favorite of teachers portrays food chains of varying lengths, but they all start with the green plant.

Mighty Mole and Super Soil—Below your feet, Mighty Mole is on the move. Like a swimmer through dirt, she strokes through the soil and introduces your readers to this vital underground ecosystem.

More Nature Awareness Books from Dawn Publications

Wonderful Nature, Wonderful You—Nature can be a great teacher. With a light touch especially suited to children, this 20th Anniversary edition evokes feelings of calm acceptance, joy, and wonder.

Over in the Forest: Come and Take a Peek—Children learn the ways of common forest animals and count their babies, all to the rhythm of the traditional tune "Over in the Meadow."

A Moon of My Own—An adventurous young girl journeys around the world, if only in her dreams. She discovers natural beauty and manmade wonders, accompanied by her companion—the moon.

There's a Bug on My Book—Children's imaginations will be engaged as they're introduced to all sorts of critters that hop, fly, wiggle, and slide across the pages of this book.

Dawn Publications is dedicated to inspiring in children a deeper understanding and appreciation for all life on Earth. You can browse through our titles, download resources for teachers, and order at www.dawnpub.com or call 800-545-7475.